It's All In How You Look At It!

Keeping Perspective on Life's Ups and Downs

Inspired by Faith

It's All in How You Look At It!
ISBN 978-0-9828555-7-7

Published by Product Concept Mfg., Inc.
2175 N. Academy Circle #200, Colorado Springs, CO 80909

©2011 Product Concept Mfg., Inc. All rights reserved.

Written and Compiled by Patricia Mitchell
in association with Product Concept Mfg., Inc.

All scripture quotations are from the King James version
of the Bible unless otherwise noted.

Scriptures taken from the Holy Bible,
New International Version®, NIV®.
Copyright © 1973, 1978, 1984, 2010 by Biblica, Inc.™
Used by permission of Zondervan.
All rights reserved worldwide.
www.zondervan.com

It's All*in How You Look At it!

Ever notice how some people

seem untouched by life's strains and stresses? No matter when you see them, they seem relaxed and happy.

Meet them in the dentist's office five minutes before their root canal, and you'd think they're about to go on a picnic. While they're busy scraping an inch of ice off their windshield, they're thanking God for a wonderful day.

Umbrella in hand, they're dancing around the silver lining while the rest of us are gaping in dismay at the oncoming cloud.

It's not magic (and not rocket science, either). It's a choice...a choice you can make. A choice to stop stressing. To be happy. To enjoy the journey.

It's all in how you look at it.

OPTIMISM

Something great is up ahead!

A Case for Clichés

There's a veritable clutch of clichés to "help" you when you're down. "When life gives you lemons," a friend gleefully crows, "make lemonade!" But truth be told, you've always thought the popular summer beverage came in a carton from your grocery store. You don't make it – you pour it.

"There's a silver lining to this thing," another friend confidently intones. Exactly what that silver lining might be remains vague. You're assured, however, that the silver lining exists.

Yet the old sayings express a core truth. In life's many and varied circumstances—especially the tough ones—you can find the seeds of positive change and new opportunities. They may not be obvious, but they're well worth the search.

The secret of being optimistic begins with the unshakable belief that something good—even beautiful—can come out of your present situation. And that's what makes you put your head up and smile.

Bushel of lemons? Clouds in the sky?
Maybe a problem...or maybe not.

What's a dull day but a time to discover the simple pleasures of life...

What's a routine job but an opportunity to perform it extraordinarily well...

What's a barrier but a challenge to prove you can overcome it...

What's an impossible to-do list but a chance to establish your priorities...

What's a friend but the privilege of being there for someone else...

What's a frustrating day but an invitation
to practice kindness under pressure...

What's a quiet evening but a chance to
lose yourself in a good book...

What's a crowd but the occasion of
sharing a smile...a greeting...
a helping hand to someone in need...

It's all in how you look at it!

Hope, like the gleaming taper's light,
Adorns and cheers our way;
And still, as darker grows the night,
Emits a brighter ray.
Oliver Goldsmith

Be still, and know that I am God.
Psalm 46:10

Optimism: A cheerful frame of
mind that enables a tea kettle to
sing though it's in hot water up to
its nose.

Hope itself is a species of happiness,
and, perhaps, the chief happiness
which this world affords.
Samuel Johnson

No one has ever ruined his eyes by
looking on the sunny side of life.

GET GOING

Sometimes I just need a nudge
in the right direction.

Don't Stop Now!

So you think you're stalled? Consider these famous "failures":

He experienced two job losses, failed in several campaigns for public office, and suffered bouts of poor physical and emotional health. Obstacles? Yes. Barriers? No. Through hard work, a focus on the successes that came to him, and an enduring belief in the future Abraham Lincoln became one of our nation's most revered presidents.

Her boyfriend died on the battlefield in World War I, and later in her first marriage she suffered spousal abuse. She resigned from her job as a journalist after an ankle injury. Though she finished her novel in 1929, it was repeatedly rejected by editors and not published until 1936. "Gone With the Wind" author Margaret Mitchell refused to allow personal setbacks to destroy her belief in herself or her abilities.

His first animated film company, Laugh-O-Grams, went bankrupt when he ran out of money. The failure prompted him to move from Kansas City to Holly-wood, where he joined with his brother and started another production company. Talent, enthusiasm, and faith in his dreams made Walt Disney a house-hold name.

Change Is Good

If God had intended everything to stay the same, He wouldn't have created winter...spring...summer...and fall. He wouldn't have caused the tide to ebb and flow, nor the moon to wax and wane. He wouldn't have let morning become day, nor day become night, nor night become morning again.

If everything stayed the same, a seed would remain a seed...an acorn would keep on being an acorn...a root would never deepen and spread. Flowers would never have reason to grow.

If everything stayed the same, there would be no weeping...but no laughter. No failings...but no dreams come true. No breaking down...but no building up. No passing of life...but no babies born into it.

If everything stayed the same... but thank God, it doesn't.

You didn't fail.

You haven't lost.

Instead, you've gained...

...a chance to start again, this time
with new ideas, new energy,
and a new perspective.

...an opportunity to try something
you've always wanted to do
without the ties of the past to
restrict you.

...a time to step back, take it easy for a while, and let fresh plans take shape in your mind and heart.

...a space in your life for renewal and reflection.

...an occasion to reach out to others who can help and encourage you.

It's all in how you look at it!

The bills are coming at me
from both sides!

A Little Short?

What a blessing it would be to not need to think about money! Or would it? Money is a gift from God intended for our use. If we had so much we never had to think about it, we would take it for granted. Money would gain the power to control us and lose the power to teach us:

- Moderation. Because we have a set amount of money to spend, we know not to buy on impulse and to avoid needless purchases. Added bonus: our lives are not over-stuffed with stuff!

- Compassion. Knowing what it's like to be short of money gives us a glimpse into the lives of those who are without money. Perhaps that's why so many middle- and lower-income earners are also generous givers.

- Innovation. A need for additional income leads us to use our skills and talents, broaden our education, and pursue new opportunities. Consider how much more than money our work provides, yet how little our motivation to work if it weren't for the money we earn.

- Independence. We're not as easily lured by advertising when a limited income compels us to watch our spending. When we pause to think through the real benefits of products, we make choices independent of catchy ads.

- Decision-making. A finite amount of money leads us to set priorities. What we buy and don't is a good indication of what we truly value.

- Simplicity. There's satisfaction in knowing what we can live without. There's peace in not needing more, more, more.

U.S. Bills

The first paper money for public use in the United States was printed in 1862 during the Civil War. Each bill, called a greenback for the ink color used, was hand-signed by one of six people working in the basement of the Treasury building. By the end of the War, however, over one-third of the paper money in circulation was counterfeit!

Those first bills came in denominations of 1 cent, 5 cents, 25 cents, and 50 cents. One hundred years later, you could put $1,000, $5,000 and $10,000 bills in your wallet! These large bills are no longer printed and rarely used anymore, due to the prevalence of check, internet, and credit-card transactions. They're still legal tender, though...and any way you look at it, it would be nice to have a few of those whopper bills set aside for a rainy day!

Did you know…

If you're having an argument with your spouse, it's more than likely the subject is money. Why? Because our attitude toward money is determined by family background, personal experience, and our perceived needs and wants. Two otherwise compatible people can hold strong, but opposing, views on the topic!

Your priority might be to save for the future, but your spouse believes in enjoying it now. You want to use an unexpected windfall as a down payment on a bigger house, while your spouse would rather pay off the house you're currently living in. You may not see the necessity of keeping a strict budget, but your spouse wants to track every penny.

Whether you're one of a couple or a single person, it's a good idea to clarify what money means to you and what you expect it to do.

The Good Book
on Good Money Management

Keep your lives free from the love of money
and be content with what you have.
Hebrews 13:5 NIV

For the love of money is a root of all kinds
of evil. Some people, eager for money,
have wandered from the faith and pierced
themselves with many griefs.
1 Timothy 6:10 NIV

No one can serve two masters...
You cannot serve both God and money.
Matthew 6:24 NIV

Labour not to be rich.
Proverbs 23:4

Then he said to them, "Watch out!
Be on your guard against all kinds of greed;
life does not consist in an abundance
of possessions."
Luke 12:15 NIV

Suppose one of you wants to build a tower.
Won't you first sit down and estimate the
cost to see if you have enough money to
complete it?
Luke 14:28 NIV

Seek ye first the kingdom of God,
and his righteousness; and all these
things shall be added unto you.
Matthew 6:33

YOU'RE AS YOUNG AS YOU FEEL

Age can't keep
me down!

Of a Certain Age

As Mark Twain once said, "Wrinkles should merely indicate where smiles have been." And where smiles still are! No matter your age, nothing lights up your face like a generous, natural, from-the-heart smile.

As the number of candles on top of your birthday cake increase, so will the wrinkles on your face. You'll notice a few thin lines at first, and unless you're inclined toward cosmetic surgery or other procedures, these few lines eventually invite their deeper friends and relatives to join them.

Then one day, in front the mirror, you have to admit it – you've got wrinkles.

So now what? You can either slather your face with three layers of cake make-up and wear turtle-neck shirts, or...

...be the proud possessor of a face radiating real-life experience and worldly knowledge. Wisdom, even.

...be thankful you've lived so many years and have so many sweet memories of things you've seen and done.

...be willing to let your genuine self come through in the sparkle of your eyes, the kindness of your smile, and the gentleness of your voice...and no one will notice the lines on your face.

...be a good example of how to age gracefully for those who have not yet earned their share of wrinkles!

Smile Lines

In the beginning God made a man and a woman, and He set them on Earth. Then the man and the woman looked at each other and burst out laughing.
African saying

Age is an issue of mind over matter.
If you don't mind, it doesn't matter.
Mark Twain

The happiest people seem to be those who have no particular reason for being happy except that they are so.
W. R. Inge

I'd like to grow very old as slowly as possible.
Charles Lamb

To Everything a Season

The beauty of each season,
the blessing of each day,
Lies in the angel-laughter
heard as children play.

It's swept up in the marvels
youthful dreams inspire—
It's captured in the magic
sealed in love's desire.

It's in the smile of wisdom,
in contentment's art—
There's beauty in each season
whispered to the heart.

Patricia Mitchell

There is no duty we so much
underrate as the duty of being happy.
Robert Louis Stevenson

Be willing to have it so.
Acceptance of what has happened
is the first step to overcoming the
consequences of any misfortune.
William James

No one can make you feel inferior
without your consent.
Eleanor Roosevelt

The Constitution only guarantees the
American people the right to pursue
happiness. You have to catch it yourself.
Benjamin Franklin

I make the most of all that comes
and the least of all that goes.
Sara Teasdale

TRAMPLED FEELINGS?

Moving right along...

Horsing Around?

A friend made a hurtful comment, but you ignored it. A co-worker told an offensive joke, but you let it pass. In both cases, you changed the topic as quickly as you could, and the uncomfortable moment slipped into oblivion.

Yet you can't forget the words. You can't help going back, hearing them again, wondering. Though the relationship with your friend and co-worker appears to be moving right along, something has changed. You now possess knowledge you didn't have before, and your assumptions about and feelings toward two people are different than they were before.

Among friends, family members, and co-workers, offenses are bound to occur. Even our closest loved ones may see things from a point of view, a perspective, or a vantage point different than our own. Or they might be just horsing around, never imagining their words could sting. Offense often lies in the ears of the hearer.

To truly move forward in any relationship, however, means you cannot keep looking backward. It means treating tender wounds now, before they become aching sores.

Use their words and your reaction as a springboard to a stronger and more honest relationship. In a private conversation, talk about how the words sounded to you and describe why you were hurt to hear them. Only if you are willing to speak with honesty and clarity will your relationships continue to move forward in a meaningful, joyful way.

Wounded by words?

Now you have the opportunity to...

Forge a deeper friendship by revealing your heartfelt thoughts honestly, truthfully, and kindly.

Own your reactions by exploring why you feel the way you do and what part your personal experiences and biases play in your feelings.

Reach out with an open hand, realizing we are all human. We all make mistakes. We all speak words we wish we could reclaim.

Grow in understanding...in knowing
more about the intricacies, the give and take,
of all our relationships. Gain wisdom,
and with it, grace among all people.

Invest in your emotional health by
being willing to stand up for yourself...
to shun the snare of anger and bitterness...
to express your point of view in
a calm and respectful way.

Vow to listen to others and hear
their response to your words.
Readily accept their apology.

End with a smile...a clasp of hands...
a hug. Begin again, moving forward
with genuine affection.

It's all in how you look at it!

Words To Live By
And To Forgive By

Better by far you should forget
and smile, than you should
remember and be sad.
Christina Rossetti

A joke never turns an enemy
to a friend, but often turns
a friend into an enemy.
Proverb

It's not what happens to you,
but how you react to it that matters.
Epictetus

He who forgives ends the quarrel.
African Proverb

Always do right—this will gratify
some and astonish the rest.
Mark Twain

Life is better when shared.

The Real Adventure

One climbs high mountains, while the other explores dense jungles. One chases notorious criminals and brings them to justice, while the other performs dangerous stunts in front of cheering crowds.

Certainly, most of us would say these people live adventurous lives! Yet life's real adventure lies closer to home. It rests as near as a friend, partner, companion, or spouse.

We embark on this adventure the moment we open ourselves to another person...when we reveal a hope, ask for help, admit a wrong, speak our mind, or share a dream. These are the everyday adventures that require not steel-will, derring-do, and a big dose of adrenalin, but a humble willingness to make ourselves vulnerable.

Vulnerability takes courage—after all, we might get hurt, or be disappointed or let down. True! That's what makes being vulnerable an adventure. After all, if the mountains were not high, what risk would there be in climbing them? If the jungle held no danger, what boldness would it take to explore it? In any true adventure, there's risk.

Is it possible at this time of life...after everything...at this age and in this place for you to live adventurously?

Adventure is ...

Giving your most precious
possession—your time—to another.

Revealing your hopes, dreams,
and aspirations to another.

Offering your gifts and blessings
to help another.

Admitting your weaknesses
to another.

Opening your heart to another.

Walking alongside another,
even when the road is rough.

Communicating kindly and
truthfully with another.

Being genuinely interested in
another's thoughts and feelings.

Comforting, encouraging,
and helping another.

Sharing everyday blessings,
for in sharing they are doubled.

This is true adventure.

Along the Line of Friendship

If you do a huge favor for a friend then
never see her again, it was still worth it.

Welcome trouble: it's the only way
you'll find out who your true friends are.

Love is blind, while friendship
simply closes its eyes.

Friends are the angels we spend time
with here on earth.

Only your real friends will tell you
when you have lettuce stuck between
your teeth.

One loyal friend is worth
ten thousand relatives.
Euripides

'Tis the privilege of friendship
to talk nonsense, and have her
nonsense respected.
Charles Lamb

Friendship is like money,
easier made than kept.
Samuel Butler

HANG ON!

God is
everywhere...
even at your
wit's end.

Now Is the Time

It's something you never imagined happening, and you didn't see it coming. Now you feel like the foundation of your life has crumbled under your feet, and no wonder. It has. Things aren't what they used to be!

There's no better time than now to start building something new.

While much good may be gone, no doubt there were things about the past that you didn't like...things you may have wanted to change, but didn't or couldn't. Now is the time to turn over a new leaf...to express a part of yourself long put aside...to reach out and embrace life afresh.

Now is the time to accept a new reality...to redefine "normal"...to reclaim yourself...to look with expectant eyes at what today and the days ahead have to offer.

Now is the time to realistically assess your situation...the good and the bad, the opportunities and the challenges. If you have trouble seeing your way clearly, talk these things over with a loved one, close friend, or counselor.

Remember: Though much has changed, not everything needs to be changed. Today is the day to focus on necessary decisions. Make those, and leave all other decisions until tomorrow.

Now is the time to care for your physical, emotional, and spiritual health. Refuse to let avoidable illness or stress drain your energy, because...

... there's no better time than now to start building something new.

Building Blocks for a New Foundation

Take Time
Well-being is attained little by little,
and nevertheless is no little thing itself.
Zeno of Citium

Visualize
What an immense power over the life is
the power of possessing distinct aims.
The voice, the dress, the look, the very
motion of a person, define and alter when
he or she begins to live for a reason.
Elizabeth Stuart Phelps

Own the Day
Have regular hours for work and play;
make each day both useful and pleasant,
and prove that you understand the worth
of time by employing it well. Then youth
will be delightful, old age will bring few
regrets, and life will become a beautiful
success.
Louisa May Alcott

Step Forward

The man who insists upon seeing with
perfect clearness before he decides,
never decides.
Henri-Frédéric Amiel

Even if you're on the right track,
you'll get run over if you just sit there.
Will Rogers

To tend, unfailingly, unflinchingly,
towards a goal, is the secret of success.
Anna Pavlova

We cannot do everything at once,
but we can do something at once.
Calvin Coolidge

Believe

To believe in the things you can see and touch is no belief at all; but to believe in the unseen is a triumph and a blessing.
Abraham Lincoln

Let us remember that within us there is a palace of immense magnificence.
Teresa of Avila

Believe that life is worth living and your belief will help create the fact.
William James

Deliverance

Reach out...
for hands to **help**
for words of **hope**
for comfort's
healing balm.

Reach in...
for eyes to **see**
for life's **rebirth**
for soul's
renewing calm.

We're all in this together.

Strength in Numbers

Once upon a time, there was a farmer who had 12 sons. Not one son could get along with his brother. Day after day they argued and fought.

The farmer grew tired of hearing one son's story contradict the story of another, and the boys' constant bickering wearied him. He couldn't sleep for the anguish he suffered over the foolish disputes of his sons.

Then one day he had an idea. He collected 12 stout sticks from the field and tied the sticks tightly together. That evening after supper, he asked his sons to stay at the table and listen to what he had to say.

"Sons," the farmer said, placing the bound sticks in front of him. "I want each one of you to come, from the youngest to the eldest, and break this bundle of sticks with your bare hands."

From the youngest to the eldest, each son tried. None succeeded.

Then the farmer said to the eldest, "Unloose the bundle and take one stick. Give one to each of your brothers, and keep one for yourself." When each boy held a stick, the farmer said, "See if you can break it now." The twelve sticks easily broke.

"This is what I want to tell you," their father said. "Alone, you are weak. You are breakable. But bound together in love and loyalty, you are strong. No one could snap your spirit or break anything you decide to do."

If you were meant to go it alone, then God wouldn't have put so many good people into your life.

Some to walk ahead of you to light the way, and some to walk beside you to hold your hand.

And some to walk behind you, learning from your example.

Some to encourage you when you're feeling down, and some to help lighten the load.

Some to simply shine a smile in the middle of a gloomy day.

Some to celebrate with you and rejoice in your success when good things come... some to comfort you when life's hardships and losses knock at your door.

Some to enter your life for a season, and some to be your friend and companion on life's journey.

Some to help you up, and some who will be lifted up by you. Some to give to you, and some who will receive from you.

Some to annoy you, to test you, to challenge you, to frustrate you. Some to show you your measure of patience, kindness, and gentleness.

All to travel with you on this amazing, adventurous, joyous journey called life.

We need one another because…

What do we live for; if it is not to make life less difficult for each other?
George Eliot

No man is an island, entire of itself.
John Donne

Two are better than one, because they have a good reward for their labour. For if they fall, the one will lift up his fellow.
Ecclesiastes 4:9,10

Trouble shared is trouble halved.
Dorothy Sayers

Everything that lives—
lives not alone,
nor for itself.
William Blake

Alone we can do so little;
together we can do so much.
Helen Keller

Keep
Looking
up!

Expect the Best

Two people, witnessing the same incident, often offer conflicting versions of what took place. Neither is a liar, and neither is trying to change the facts. It's simply that they're viewing the scene from two different vantage points.

In a similar way, you are a witness of your life. What you say about it – your past experiences, your current situation, your prospects for the future – depend not so much on what has happened, but on where you're standing while you describe it.

Some people assess their life while standing in the shadows. They'll tell you about the teacher who punished them unfairly in pre-school, the grade they didn't deserve, the job they didn't get, the friend who let them down, and so on...and on...and on.

Yes, they're telling the truth. Bad things happened, but bad things happen to everyone. In the shadows, however, that's all they see.

Other people look at life while standing in the sunshine. They'll tell you about the subject they loved in school, the excitement of going on their first airplane ride, an out-of-the-blue kindness of a stranger...and what a delight to listen to them!

And they're telling the truth. Good things happened, because good things happen to everyone. Sunshine serves to highlight them.

When people ask you about your past, where do you stand? When people ask you how your day is going, where do you stand? As you look to the future, where do you stand – in the gloomy shadows, or in the brilliant sunshine?

Positive thoughts…

…lead to productive words and actions.

…bring about a cheerful, upbeat attitude.

…bolster self-image and confidence.

…heal the heart and soothe the soul.

…expect that good things
are just around the corner.

…reveal strength of character
and self-control.

...affect others for the better.

...determine success
   in discovering opportunity.

...brighten the face and lighten the step.

...furnish a joyful, carefree spirit.

It's all in how you look at it!

10 Ways to Being Positive

1. Decide to be happy.
2. Recite a positive and meaningful affirmation of life every day.
3. Focus on things that are going well.
4. Banish negative or depressing thoughts.
5. Smile and offer a friendly greeting to everyone you see.

6. Make the best of problems
   that come your way.
7. Put others in the best possible light.
8. Speak gently, kindly, and thoughtfully.
9. Be thankful for your blessings.
10. Nurture faith, hope, and love.

Don't worry.

If there
isn't a path,
we'll
make
one.

Which Way?

You're at a crossroads in life, and there's not a clear-cut path ahead. In fact, you could go in one of several directions. Each path presents its own advantages and disadvantages, and none offers a guaranteed outcome.

No one has left you a road map.

If you're like many people, you're feeling anxious and somewhat confused. You're tempted to do nothing, yet you realize that doing nothing is itself a chosen path—a path leading to nowhere you want to go.

If you're one of a few brave souls, you're feeling exhilarated. This is just the way you like it! Now you get to make your own way, pick your own direction, and discover your own happiness! You're tempted to move, and move quickly, down the path that promises adventure, excitement, and fulfillment, but you know it's a path best taken with forethought and preparation.

Most of us are somewhere in between. Out of our comfort zone, we're a little shaken, but at the same time exhilarated by the chance to explore new options...to look at new scenery...walk a new path, perhaps one that no one has taken before.

The Road Not Taken

Two roads diverged in a yellow wood,
And sorry I could not travel both
And be one traveler, long I stood
And looked down one as far as I could
To where it bent in the undergrowth;

Then took the other, as just as fair,
And having perhaps the better claim,
Because it was grassy and wanted wear;
Though as for that the passing there
Had worn them really about the same,

And both that morning equally lay
In leaves no step had trodden black.
Oh, I kept the first for another day!
Yet knowing how way leads on to way,
I doubted if I should ever come back.

I shall be telling this with a sigh
Somewhere ages and ages hence:
Two roads diverged in a wood, and I—
I took the one less traveled by,
And that has made all the difference.

Robert Frost

Essentials for the Journey

A destination in mind. State your goal in as few words as possible and as specifically as you can. Write it down and keep it in front of you. Memorize it, so when someone asks you, "Say, what are you doing these days?" you can answer with clarity and confidence.

Feet on the ground. Take the first step... and then the next...and then the next. Your goal remains a distant dream until you do what it takes to make it reality. Sure, you might make a few wrong turns, but that's OK. It means you're moving and learning!

An eye for opportunity. Remain open, flexible, and teachable. Uncharted paths provide unexpected opportunities. It's up to you to see them and use them, even if they're things you hadn't considered before.

A heart for adventure. Enjoy the journey. Talk about your discoveries, what's working for you and what isn't. Determine that the path you've chosen will be exciting, enlightening, and a whole lot of fun!

It's all in how you look at it.

I call him my opportunity
to practice patience.

Difficult People

Experts tell us that healthy and supportive relationships are essential to our emotional well-being and positively affect our physical health. So important are good relationships, many claim, that we need to eliminate the difficult ones.

Trouble is, we can't always refuse to see, visit, meet, or work with someone whose personality and mannerisms drive us to distraction. We remove a spouse, family member, or longtime friend from our lives only at a high emotional cost to ourselves. The more we avoid others, the more isolated we become...and the more unhappy.

So let's face it. As long as we're among people, some are going to rub us the wrong way. Others are going to prove downright frustrating. The wider our social circle, the more often we will face difficult people...and the more opportunities we will have to learn how to respond to them with grace and goodwill.

It's all in how you look at it.

The Care and Feeding of Relationships

Sow the seeds of kindness, even among
the thorns. In the marvelous, miraculous,
and wondrous soil of the human heart,
even thorns have blossomed.

Cultivate the soil, searching for
good qualities...the new shoot,
the opening bud, the green leaf...
and mark these things.

Shield yourself from the storms
of criticism, anger, and negativism with
self-control, understanding, and wisdom.

Nurture forgiveness at the center of your
heart, and let the fragrance of its fruit
refresh your spirit.

Loosen the dried, packed dirt of blame
and defensiveness, old offenses and
rehashed arguments...amend with
listening, thinking, compassion,
and understanding.

Prune revenge from your thoughts,
words, and actions...control the only
one you can control: yourself.

Sprinkle liberally with kind and gentle
humor...pour out the sunshine of
forgiveness and love.

Count to Ten

1. I can choose to change my response.

2. I can ask myself if I'm overreacting.

3. I can see myself from where the other stands.

4. I can listen.

5. I can understand.

6. I can perceive unspoken needs and hurts.

7. I can seek help and counsel.

8. I can temper my expectations.

9. I can refuse to wound.

10. I can rise above the situation.

You can.

It's all in how you look at it.

It's a balancing act.

Prioritizing

You've heard the proverb: "All work and no play makes Jack a dull boy." But you may not be aware of its sequel: "All play and no work makes Jack a mere toy."

Keeping a healthy balance between work and rest is a challenge. For most of us, work takes up almost all our waking hours, leaving precious little time for ourselves. As we dash past our slower-paced friends, we wish we had an hour of their free, unstructured time.

Yet life in the slow lane can fall out of balance, too. If we spend no time engaged in purposeful, challenging, and productive activity, boredom sets in. We feel as if we're simply spinning our wheels and going nowhere.

God made us with the capacity to work...do... think...create, and it's as much a part of us as our need for rest and relaxation.

For you, have the last 24 hours been all work and no play...or all play and no work?

You can complain...or change. Keep all work or all play...or balance both.

A time to every purpose under the heaven.

Ecclesiastes 3:1

A time to be alone...
and a time to reach out to others.

A time to focus on work, duty,
and responsibilities...
and a time to rest, renew, and refresh.

A time to enthusiastically agree...
and a time to respectfully disagree.

A time to reminisce about the past...
a time to plan for the future...
and a time to revel in the pleasure
of the present moment.

A time to understand...
and a time to be understood.

There is time for caution...
and a time for courage.

A time for sorrow...
and a time for happiness.

A time for words...
and a time for silence.

A time for waking...
and a time for dreams.

There is time.

It's all in how you use it.

Life is like...

...riding a bicycle
Life is like riding a bicycle. To keep your balance you must keep moving.
Albert Einstein

...a good armchair
What I dream of is an art of balance, of purity and serenity devoid of troubling or depressing subject matter—a soothing, calming influence on the mind, rather like a good armchair which provides relaxation from physical fatigue.
Henri Matisse

...a gamble

Life will always remain a gamble, with
prizes sometimes for the imprudent,
and blanks so often to the wise.

Jerome K. Jerome

...a feather bed and a tightrope

Life is always a tightrope or a feather bed.
Give me the tightrope.

Edith Wharton

TOO MUCH WHINING

Some people see the cheese —
some see the hole.

The Rumble of Grumble

The story describes a remote monastery with extraordinarily strict rules. One rule stipulates that monks maintain silence at all times, except every second year. At that time and at that time only, monks have permission to speak two words.

A young man joins the order. At the end of his first two years, he approaches his superior and utters his allotted two words. "Bad food," he said.

At the end of his second two years, he appears before his superior and delivers two more words. "Lumpy bed."

At the end of his third two years, he stands in front of his superior and announces: "I quit!"

"I'm certainly not surprised," his superior replies. "Ever since you've been here, all you've done is complain."

In two words, describe your day. A complaint... or a blessing?

What Could Be Better?

At a staff meeting, an office manager set up two white boards for all to see. At the top of one, he wrote:

Things That Went Right

At the top of the other, he wrote:

Things That Could Have Been Better

First, he invited staff members to call out their successes...the goals reached, products shipped, profits earned, customer compliments received.

Then the manager turned to the second board. Here he asked staff members to name things that could have been better. Things that, had they to do over again, they would do more efficiently and more effectively. Things that turned out not quite the way they wanted. Things that could be better...and with time and effort, will be.

Put complaints in their proper perspective by giving first place to your triumphs and successes. Turn your complaints into problems that have solutions by calling them "Things That Could Have Been Better." That's what they are, because you're going to work toward making them that way.

LAUGH AT IT

There has been much tragedy in my life;
at least half of it actually happened.

Mark Twain

CHOOSE IT

It is no use to grumble and complain;
It's jest as cheap and easy to rejoice;
When God sorts out the weather and
sends rain. Why, rain's my choice.

James Whitcomb Riley

FIND IT

Sweet are the uses of adversity,
Which, like the toad, ugly and
venomous, Wears yet a precious
jewel in his head.

William Shakespeare

Bad time, hard times—this is what people keep saying; but let us live well, and times shall be good. We are the times: Such as we are, such are the times.
Augustine

Be glad of life because it gives you the chance to love and to work and to play and to look up at the stars.
Henry Van Dyke

To a brave man, good and bad luck are like his right and left hand. He uses both.
Catherine of Siena

Friends come in all shapes and sizes.

Good Impressions

We decide, in less than a minute of meeting someone new, whether the person is nice or not nice...interesting or uninteresting...a potential friend or forgettable acquaintance.

But if we make a conscious decision to set aside snap judgements in favor of a more thoughtful assessment, the time and effort may be worth it.

You may find a life-enhancing friend in someone who doesn't look like you...who doesn't share all your beliefs and perceptions...who has lived life in a whole other world until your paths crossed.

A warm smile and a friendly remark may reveal someone who can tell a delightful and amusing story, but who has trouble initiating conversation. An inviting question might open another person's vast knowledge and know-how to you...a passionate enthusiast who was just waiting to be asked.

Yes, friends come in all shapes, sizes, ages, and colors, and they come from all backgrounds. No matter how different we look to one another, however, we all share these things in common:

We all have hopes and dreams...
goals and experiences...
loves, joys, and wisdom about life
from one corner of the world.
We all have stories to tell.
It's all in your willingness to look more than once.

A Story of Friendship

Why should I have paid attention to her? I was popular, head of the class, the girl everyone wanted to hang out with. She was the new girl in the school.

She was sweet, but plain. She didn't dress the way people in my circle did, and she never would – she couldn't afford it. So, even though we had classes together and the same homeroom all year, I didn't pay attention to her.

At our ten-year class reunion, I saw her again. I had had a rough time since leaving school – my marriage had ended, and I was a single mom raising three children. I worked two jobs to make ends meet. Most of my friends had great careers, successful marriages, and were living in expensive new homes and condos.

Readers, I'm sure you can see this coming. She hadn't changed much – there was nothing fancy about her – but she possessed something special I had never noticed before.

I saw it when she came up to me and greeted me. Her eyes were kind, and her words were welcoming and warm. We started talking. She reminded me that we were in art class together...a class that inspired her to become an art teacher. Our conversation reminded me how long it had been since I had picked up a paint brush...and how much I missed it.

We promised to meet for coffee the following week.

I wish I had looked a little closer a long time ago.

Appearances

How little do they see what is, who
frame their hasty judgments upon
that which seems.
Robert Southey

Judge not according to the appearance,
but judge righteous judgment.
John 7:24

Half the work that is done in this world is
to make things appear what they are not.
Elias Root Beadle

The bosom can ache beneath diamond
brooches; and many a blithe heart
dances under coarse wool.
Edwin Hubbel Chapin

Man looks at the outward appeareance,
but the LORD looks at the heart.
1 Samuel 16:7 NIV

A Must-Have Accessory–
Humor

A person without a sense of humor is like a wagon without springs. It's jolted by every pebble on the road.
Henry Ward Beecher

Good humor is one of the best articles of dress one can wear in society.
William Thackeray

A merry heart maketh a cheerful countenance.
Proverbs 15:13

Humor is the great thing, the saving thing. The minute it crops up, all our irritations and resentments slip away and a sunny spirit takes their place.
Mark Twain

A merry heart doeth good like a medicine.
Proverbs 17:22

I have this really bad feeling.

That Looming Feeling

Some things stand like an "elephant in the room" of your mind. They fill your thoughts with dread, like the fear of losing a job...anxiety concerning a medical condition...worry about a loved one or a cherished relationship.

There's nothing you can do to move the "elephant" out of your life, because it's there and it refuses to budge. The only practical option is to look at it right in the face...to stare it down to size.

First, describe the beast. Use as few words as possible, and be specific. Quite often, accurately naming the problem leads to its solution.

Second, devise an action plan. Action might consist of spending time in prayer...picturing a good outcome...getting advice from others...following up on medical check-ups and tests...opening a frank discussion with supervisors...sharing your concerns with others.

Third, if the "elephant" still threatens to fill the room, enlarge the room. Bring in other people to help you manage your fears. Find other interests to take your mind off the situation. Put it in perspective.

The rooms of your heart, mind, and spirit are far bigger than any elephant.

BIG TROUBLE:

When **"IT"** enters your life...

...do not deny It. It has happened to people from the beginning of time... to good people, to people who don't deserve It. To people like you.

When **"IT"** enters your life...

...control what you can control. You can control your response and reactions... your actions and attitude. You cannot chase It out of your life, but you can accept It...learn to co-exist with It... even discover some good in It...find how It enhances your understanding, your compassion, your faith.

When **"IT"** enters your life...

...refuse to let It define you. You have a name and an identity outside of It...you have interests and passions beyond the reach of It...you are tougher, stronger, and nobler than It will ever be. And you are loved.

When **"IT"** enters your life...

...live joyfully anyway. If you can no longer run a marathon because of It, use your voice to cheer others on. If there are days you cannot get out of bed because of It, send your warmest thoughts to those you love and care about. If you are no longer doing what you used to do because of It, put your hands to something new.

Fear makes the wolf bigger than it is.
German Proverb

I am not afraid of storms for I am
learning how to sail my ship.
Louisa May Alcott

The only way round is through.
Robert Frost

Nothing is so much to be feared as fear.
Henry David Thoreau

You can never cross the ocean unless
you have the courage to lose sight of
the shore.
Christopher Columbus

Where there is peace and meditation,
then there is neither anxiety nor doubt.
Francis of Assisi

Those who suffer he delivers in their suffering; he speaks to them in their affliction.
Job 36:15 NIV

In the world ye shall have tribulation: but be of good cheer; I have overcome the world.
John 16:33

Comfort yourselves together, and edify one another.
1 Thessalonians 5:11

Come to me, all you who are weary and burdened, and I will give you rest.
Matthew 11:28 NIV

Who of you by worrying can add a single hour to his life?
Matthew 6:27 NIV

Is there more catnip for me over there?

A Modern Fable

There were two men who invested $10,000 each, and their money doubled in a short amount of time. They happily slapped each other on the back, and each man went his way.

The first man was thankful to have received such a gift. For his $10,000, he chose a low-risk investment that stood to yield a moderate return over time. And it did. The man was glad for the extra income it gave him, and he shared his money with those less fortunate.

The second man was dazzled by the amount that came his way, and he immediately set about to get even more. He chose risky high-yield investments, and as money poured in, he sought out even bigger returns. He believed he possessed a golden touch.

At the end of 25 years, the two men met again. The first man said how grateful he was for the blessings his investment had made possible. The second man boasted about how much he was making, and, knowing his friend's investment returned so much less, pitied him.

At the end of 35 years, the men met once more. By then the stock market had crashed and both men's investments were now worth exactly $1. The first man smiled and said he was satisfied, as he had been able to help so many people for so many years. Then he handed his remaining dollar to the second man, who was weeping inconsolably.

He who is content can never be ruined.

Looking Over the Fence

If you find someone living
like a king, do not envy him
until you know how well
he sleeps at night...
how well his spirit rests.

If you see someone
who has won a fortune,
pause before you ask
an equal share
and find out if her
newfound wealth
has brought her happiness.

If you know someone
who seems to have it all,
do not strive to match him
thing for thing
until you're sure his
conscience is at peace
and free from blame.

But if you meet
someone who's rich
in the luxuries of laughter,
warmth, and love...
then do not envy, friend
...but follow, learn,
and possess the same.

If you lose your possessions,
you've lost a lot.

If you lose your health,
you've lost a great deal.

But if you lose your peace of mind,
you've lost everything.

People with great gifts are easy to find,
but symmetrical and balanced ones never.
Ralph Waldo Emerson

Nothing is so bitter that a calm mind
cannot find comfort in it.
Seneca

I have learned, in whatsoever state I am,
therewith to be content.
Philippians 4:11

You never know what is enough unless
you know what is more than enough.
William Blake

A contented mind is the greatest blessing
a man can enjoy in this world.
Joseph Addison

WORDS ARE CHEAP

The tongue of the wise useth
knowledge aright: but the mouth
of fools poureth out foolishness.

Proverbs 15:2

Discerning Words

We can E-mail, blog, and update our website. We can call, text, or post a video. We can even pick up a pen and write a letter...or invite someone to lunch and talk face to face. Suffice it to say, we're abounding in ways to express ourselves!

With ease of communication comes a lot of communication...and where there is a plethora of words, we aren't surprised that some words are useful and some ill-spoken. Some words are meant to help and some to hurt. Some words are worthy of our attention and some best ignored.

It takes discernment to sort through all the words we hear, sifting the silly, stinging, and meaningless from the wise, productive, and true.

In the same way, it takes discernment to sift our own words before they float across our lips.

Today, words are cheap, because they're every-where. But one thing hasn't changed from the first words uttered on Earth: good words are golden.

One Good Word

One good word can

    bring together

    heal a heart

    conquer anger

    share a thought...

    lift up a spirit

    light a path

    fulfill a promise

    touch a truth.

One good word can

comfort grieving

strengthen friends

welcome strangers

mend offense...

awaken purpose

cease a strife

deliver counsel

bless a life.

Words to Live By

Violence of the tongue is very real—
sharper than any knife.
Mother Teresa

I resolve to speak ill of no man whatever,
not even in a matter of truth but rather
by some means excuse the faults I hear
charged upon others, and upon proper
occasions speak all the good I know of
everybody.
Benjamin Franklin

Talk is cheap because supply exceeds
demand.
Anonymous

Blessed is the man, who having nothing to say, abstains from giving wordy evidence of the fact.
George Eliot

Keep your remarks brief, otherwise the complete plan of your thoughts will seldom be grasped. Before you reach the conclusion, the listener will have forgotten the beginning and the middle.
Horace

A word spoken in due season, how good it is!
Proverbs 15:23

Life is
good!

A Blessing in Disguise

For many of us, the economic crisis of 2008 brought optional spending to a standstill. No more daily lattes, deli lunches, and restaurant dinners. Budgets tightened and we learned to make-do instead of buy new.

While some of us complained, others of us discovered, or rediscovered, the pleasure of a slower, simpler life. We exchanged video games for board games... take-out food for made-at-home meals... vacations abroad for time exploring our own community. We gathered for potluck dinners rather than for catered affairs, and we opted for last year's wardrobe rather than the latest trend.

Because we had found out for ourselves that money could let us down, we began to look for what would build us up. We reevaluated our priorities and plans. We reached out to friends and family with renewed appreciation, and we drew inside ourselves to find what really matters in life. We knelt down in prayer. We looked up to God.

Yes, the financial crisis brought hardship and pain to many, but it also brought with it blessings we could have known in no other way.

Secrets to the Simple (and Satisfied) Life

Cultivate friends who choose
simplicity over excess...
authenticity rather than show.

Read books that delight you...
enlighten you...enchant you.

Cook your own food...
try new recipes...
learn about spices...
try an ingredient
you've never tasted before.

Decorate with flowers you have grown...
coverlets and pillows you have made...
sayings you have penned.

Take a walk and listen to the sound of the wind through the trees...the birds in the branches...your footsteps on the path.

Sit outside. Touch the grass.
Gaze at the sky.

Read a story to a child.

Learn the names of planets and constellations...of trees on your block...of your neighbors.

Volunteer at your church...
a charity...an animal shelter...
a community organization.

Live within your means.

Be thankful.

When I dance, I dance;
when I sleep, I sleep;
yes, and when I walk alone
in a beautiful orchard,
if my thoughts have been
dwelling elsewhere,
I bring them back to the walk,
to the orchard,
to the sweetness of this solitude,
and to me.
Michel de Montaigne

To live is so startling it leaves little time
for anything else.
Emily Dickinson

Why not seize pleasure at once,
how often is happiness destroyed by
preparation, foolish preparations.
Jane Austen

The secret of happiness is not in doing
what one likes, but in liking what one
does.
James M. Barrie

God Almighty first planted a garden.
And, indeed, it is the purest of human
pleasures.
Francis Bacon

Earth's crammed with heaven.
Elizabeth Barrett Browning

Whatever is—is best.
Ella Wheeler Wilcox

I've got followers?

Here's Looking at You

Who has followers? Prominent leaders in religion, business, and politics come to mind. So do heroes and celebrities, sports stars and TV personalities. People with Twitter accounts have followers.

In truth, however, each one of us has followers. You do. Whether or not you hold a leadership position...whether or not you can claim a title in church, business, or community...whether or not you've warmed to technology... many people follow you.

Your followers are those who are influenced by your words and actions. Perhaps the counsel you offered a friend opened a whole new way of thinking for him, and he followed your advice. Perhaps the friendly hello you offered a newcomer bolstered her confidence, and she followed by greeting someone else.

Your followers are young people who see how you approach problems and handle conflict. They watch as you thoughtfully and objectively analyze issues, and they learn. When they have problems, they will follow what you did. They observe how you maintain self-control even when confronted with anger and offense, and now they know what to do when they face a similar situation. They will follow your example.

Unless you live by yourself on a deserted island, you have followers. They're friends, family members, co-workers, sales associates, and even strangers.

Fables for Leaders and Followers

THE WIND AND SUN

One day the north wind and the sun argued over who was the stronger. On seeing a man walk by, they decided to settle the matter by betting who could strip him of his coat. The wind went first, blowing and howling around the man. The man responded by wrapping his coat tightly around himself.

Then it was the sun's turn. The sun beamed down gently, embracing the man in comfort and warmth. In a few minutes, the man took off his coat and basked in her golden rays.

Gentle persuasion works better than brute force.

THE LION AND MOUSE

One day a lion came upon a mouse in the forest. Terrified, the mouse begged the lion to spare her life. The lion, out of the generosity of his heart, did so. Upon leaving, the mouse said, "If I can ever repay your kindness, Sir Lion, I will gladly do so." The lion smiled indulgently, dismissing the notion that such a small creature could ever help the king of beasts.

Many years later, the lion was caught in a trap, and ropes held him so tightly he could barely move. As it happened, the mouse came along, and hearing the lion's howls, she rushed over to him. Immediately she set to work. Gnawing furiously at the ropes, she soon snapped each one, and set the thankful lion free.

The good you do comes back to you.

THE CRAB

A mother crab constantly criticized her son for walking sideways. One day, her son asked his mother to show him how to walk straight. When the mother crab tried, she didn't succeed. When she realized that she, too, walked sideways, she stopped criticizing others for doing the same thing.

Actions speak louder than words.

THE FOX

One day a fox broke into the storeroom of a theater. As he walked between rows of costumes hanging on rods, he suddenly came upon a fearsome face glaring down at him in a menacing manner. Terrified, the fox crouched down and began his cautious retreat, and then he stopped. On second look, he realized the face was only an actor's mask.

"Ah," said the fox, very much relieved. "You appear as if you're someone to be reckoned with, but in fact, you're completely empty inside."

Outside show is no substitute for inner substance.

There's <u>always</u> something
to smile about!

From the Depths

You probably have heard a story similar to this one: A man claims he doesn't believe in God. He says he relies on himself for strength, and credits his successes to the power of his own will and intellect. Then something happens—his business fails. His health fails. His relationships slip away. He hits rock bottom. From the depths, he utters his first prayer to God.

At rock bottom or simply down in the dumps, we're in prime position to see God. When we admit our weakness, we seek His strength. When we realize the limitations of our power, we are ready to experience the infinity of His. We are ready to pray.

Our prayer can be the first step we have ever taken—or have taken in a long time—toward getting in touch with our spiritual side. Prayer is only a matter of lifting up our eyes and heart to God from wherever we are.

If the world has put you low, look up to the reality of His love. It will give you something to smile about.

When your world has turned upside down…

Remember to look across.

Reach out to those who inspire

and motivate you…

who make you feel confident and strong.

Remember to look within.

Discover the power in you.

Remember to look up.

Pray.

Hope is the thing with feathers,
That perches in the soul,
And sings the tune without the words,
And never stops at all.
Emily Dickinson

'Tis easy enough to be pleasant,
when life flows like a song.
But the man worthwhile
Is the one who will smile
When everything goes dead wrong.
Ella Wheeler Wilcox

The pure, the beautiful, the bright,
That stirred our hearts in youth,
The impulse to a wordless prayer,
The dreams of love and truth,
The longings after something lost,
The spirit's yearning cry,
The strivings after better hopes,
These things can never die.
Sarah Doudney

Turn a Frown Upside Down...
There's Always Something to
Smile About

A SMILE costs nothing but gives much. It enriches those who receive without making poorer those who give. It takes but a moment, but the memory of it sometimes lasts forever. None is so rich or mighty that he can get along without it, and none is so poor that he cannot be made rich by it.

A SMILE creates happiness in the home, fosters goodwill in business, and is the countersign of friendship. It brings rest to the weary, cheer to the discouraged, sunshine to the sad, and is nature's best antidote for trouble. Yet it cannot be bought, begged, borrowed, or stolen, for it is something that is of no value to anyone until it is given away.

SOME PEOPLE are too tired to give you a smile. Give them one of yours, as none needs a smile so much as he who has no more to give.

What's that again?

I Wonder…

Why did he make that remark? What prompted her to do what she did? When will they get their act together? Sometimes we wonder about people, and probably on more than one occasion, they have wondered about us!

Certainly one of the stumbling blocks in human relations is our wondering about one another. Is the remark controlling or caring…are her actions silly or smart…are they foolish or faithful to their own dreams?

When it comes to ourselves, we're quick to claim the second of the two choices, of course. We know our motivations and intentions, and we're certain they're good. We're not out to hurt anyone or to purposely do dumb things.

When it comes to others, however, we're apt to leap the other way. He intended to offend (really?)… she always does the wrong thing (always?)…they're obviously headed downhill (maybe…but maybe not).

When we wonder, we entertain unkind thoughts… or kind ones.

Empathy
is the art of being aware of others...
aware, because they, like you,
are human, with good intentions,
tender feelings, and cherished dreams.

Empathy
is the commitment to forgive others...
forgive, because they, like you,
have failings and careless words,
thoughtless comments escape their lips.

Empathy
is the effort to understand others...
understand, because they, like you,
are burdened with private fears and
losses buried deep within the heart.

Empathy
is the desire to reach out to others...
reach out, because they, like you,
need people to care for them and
to accept them just the way they are.

Empathy...
it's all in how you look at it.

Man has explored all
countries and all lands,
And made his own
the secrets of each clime....
Still, though he search from
shore to distant shore,
And no strange realms,
no unlocated plains
Are left for his
attainment and control,
Yet is there one more
kingdom to explore.
Go, know thyself, O man!
there yet remains
The undiscovered
country of thy soul!

Edna Wheeler Wilcox

Nothing will make us so charitable
and tender to the faults of others
as by self-examination thoroughly
to know our own.
Francois Fenelon

If you judge people, you have no
time to love them.
Mother Teresa

An humble knowledge of thyself is a
surer way to God than a deep search
after learning.
Thomas Kempis

Never criticize a man till you have
walked a mile in his shoes.
English Proverb

What lies behind us and what lies
before us are tiny matters compared
to what lies within us.
Oliver Wendell Holmes

Dare I?

Adventurous Living

"When a resolute young fellow steps up to the great bully, the world, and takes him boldly by the beard, he is often surprised to find it comes off in his hand, and that it was only tied on to scare away the timid adventurers."

Ralph Waldo Emerson's quote is worth repeating. Those "great bullies" we fear...those feelings that drag us down...those painful memories that haunt us can keep us from living a full, exciting, and satisfying life. We may have allowed the "great bully", our present adversities, to limit what we believe we are able to do and experience.

Imagine pulling the beard off the bully, despite your fear of what might happen. Imagine folding old memories, putting them in a trunk, and gently shutting the lid. Imagine turning the realities of your day to your benefit.

Imagine hiking to the summit of a mountain... or learning to sew. Imagine training for a marathon... or picking up a good book. Imagine traveling to distant lands...or spending time alone in blissful silence. Imagine living life adventurously!

What "great bullies" are holding you back? Have you ever thought of grabbing them by the beard and giving a sharp tug?

People travel to wonder at the height of the mountains, at the huge waves of the seas, at the long course of the rivers, at the vast compass of the ocean, at the circular motion of the stars, and yet they pass by themselves without wondering.

Augustine

To live content with small means;
to seek elegance rather than luxury,
and refinement rather than fashion;
to be worthy, not respectable,
and wealthy, not rich;
to listen to stars and birds,
babes and sages, with open heart;
to study hard;
to think quietly, act frankly, talk gently,
await occasions, hurry never;
in a word, to let the spiritual,
unbidden and unconscious,
grow up through the common
– this is my symphony.

William Henry Channing

I went to the woods because I wished
to live deliberately, to front only the
essential facts of life, and see if I could
not learn what it had to teach, and not,
when I came to die, discover that I had
not lived.
Henry David Thoreau

This is what you should do: Love the
earth and sun and animals, despise riches,
give alms to everyone that asks, stand
up for the stupid and crazy, devote your
income and labor to others, hate tyrants,
argue not concerning God, have patience
and indulgence toward the people...
reexamine all you have been told in
school or church or in any book, dismiss
what insults your very soul, and your
flesh shall become a great poem.
Walt Whitman

Steps to Living Adventurously

Live thankfully. When you count your blessings...your relationships, your resources, your strengths... you begin to recognize opportunities.

Live mindfully. Pay attention to the present moment. Delight in the marvels, magic, and mysteries all around you. Yes, they are there, even in the most routine of days!

Live prayerfully. God adores the sound of your voice... Talk to Him often! Prayer is our opportunity to turn every concern over to God, for he listens and cares.

Live joyfully. As the saying goes, "Live well. Laugh Often. Love much." Embrace life! Accept it. Love the adventure of it every day.

I'm having my daily dose
of bliss!